IMAGES
of Aviation

WACO

Co-founder of Waco, Clayton J. Brukner, was the driving force behind the rise to fame of the aircraft company during the two decades leading up to the Second World War. He is seen here (left) with Waco historian, Ray Brandley, standing in front of one of the classic biplanes which were produced in great numbers by the company during those dynamic and pioneering years.

IMAGES
of Aviation

WACO

Rod Simpson and Charles Trask

TEMPUS

First published 2000
Copyright © Rod Simpson and Charles Trask, 2000

Tempus Publishing Limited
The Mill, Brimscombe Port,
Stroud, Gloucestershire, GL5 2QG

ISBN 0 7524 1767 3

Typesetting and origination by
Tempus Publishing Limited
Printed in Great Britain by
Midway Clark Printing, Wiltshire

Capturing the essence of the Waco biplanes is this UPF-7 silhouetted against the clouds and acting as a reminder of the many Waco primary trainers which were used to teach American pilots during the Second World War.

Contents

Acknowledgements

Waco, its founders and its employees made a significant contribution to the development of civil aviation in the 1930s. When war came, Waco was in the forefront of pilot training and the massive production programme for the CG-4A assault gliders for the American airborne forces. First and foremost, this book is dedicated to the memory of Clayton Brukner and Sam Junkin whose vision and energy created this dynamic company and to the craftsmen in Troy, Ohio, whose products still fly in sufficient numbers to bring a thrill to their lucky owners and to aircraft enthusiasts around the world.

The photographs in this album have been selected to show the progress made by Waco from its fragile beginnings in the early 1920s to maturity in the war years. Illustrations have been drawn from the authors' collections and from the files of a number of other historians. In particular, we would like to acknowledge the help received from John M. Davis of the Wichita-based Kansas Aviation Museum which manages the photographic collection of the late Harold G. Martin. Harold Martin was Chief Photographer for Grumman for a number of years but his collection spans many aviation subjects and we have been fortunate to find many rare Waco pictures taken by him in the early post-war years. Particular thanks also go to Mike Hooks who has, once again, delved into the depths of his photo collection and has found several fascinating Waco subjects.

Details of contributed photographs are as follows. The originators of some pictures in our own collections are unknown – and we apologize to any photographers whose work has not been acknowledged. The illustrations are identified by page number with T indicating the top picture and B, the bottom one. Al Hansen 63B, M.J. Hooks 77T, 79B, 80B. Kansas Aviation Museum/Pickett Collection of Harold G. Martin 11B, 14B, 27B, 35B, 39T, 45T, 52T, 55T, 55B, 56B, 66T, 66B, 76B, 77B, 79T, 82T, 82B, 83B, 86T, 88B, 98T, 99T,101T, 101B, 105B, 108B, 110B, 112B, 113B. Gary Kuhn 84T. J. McNulty 74B. P.Trask 107T.

Rod Simpson
Charles Trask, 2000

Introduction

Created in the 1920s and 1930s, the Waco biplanes were famous in their time and are widely respected and sought after some seventy years later. Waco was, for many years, the largest manufacturer of private aircraft in the United States and its UPF-7 training biplanes and CG-4A troop-carrying gliders played a major role in the Second World War.

Like many other aircraft manufacturers, early struggles for the Waco founders brought success and furthered the development of aviation in the years following the First World War. Indeed, the foundations of the tremendously successful Waco biplane designs can be traced back to that stalwart of First World War training – the Curtiss JN-4 'Jenny'.

The late 1920s were days of growing enthusiasm for aviation. With aircraft playing such an important part in the European war the romance of aviation sparked the imagination of many. The flyers wanted to fly – and the public were enthused by flying displays, air racing and the record attempts made possible by advances in aviation technology. This was a ripe opportunity for the 'barnstorming' pilots who found an outlet for their enthusiasm together with dreams of financial gain from flying war-surplus aircraft on visits to towns around the United States. However, as the Jennies wore out, demand emerged for something better. A few of the more enterprising pilots sought to establish themselves as manufacturers.

One such wartime pilot was George E. (Buck) Weaver. His name was the basis for the Weaver Aircraft Co. which was later abbreviated to 'Waco'. Buck Weaver played only a small part in the development of the Waco Company, as he died in July 1924 long before the Waco Model 10, which was to be the core of the company's major production, was first flown. Weaver was based at Lorain, Ohio, where he and Charles Meyer carried on a precarious training and barnstorming operation using four examples of the venerable Canadian-built Curtiss JN-4 Canuck. The arrival of two aviation enthusiasts, Clayton Brukner and Elwood Junkin, at the Lorain flying field resulted in Weaver commissioning the pair to rebuild two Canucks as a starting point towards their ambitions to design and build their own light aircraft. One of Weaver's Canucks was the first recipient of the Waco name which appeared prominently on the rudder.

Brukner and Junkin had some experience of aircraft construction, having already built a small, though unsuccessful, single-seat flying boat. During the winter of 1919 to 1920, as they worked on the rebuilding of the Canucks, they conceived a new single-seat design which became known as the 'Cootie'. This was an open cockpit monoplane powered by a two-cylinder Lawrance engine and, when it was completed in February 1920, Buck Weaver was nominated as test pilot for its first flight. The Cootie flew well enough, but on the maiden flight the plane ended up in a ditch and Weaver emerged from the wreckage with facial cuts and a mutilated nose. The wreckage of the Cootie, later referred to as the Waco 1, was to re-emerge later as the Waco 2 biplane. The Waco 3 was fitted with a 30hp Henderson engine. At this point, the Weaver Aircraft Co., which had been created in 1919, abandoned the idea of a single seat 'flivver' and concentrated on developments loosely based on the familiar Jenny. This was despite considerable sales publicity for the production version of the Cootie and claims of large orders to encourage further investment in the business from outside shareholders.

The result was that the Weaver Aircraft Company needed to find a new and profitable direction and this emerged as the all-wood Waco 4. It was a considerable departure from the Curtiss JN-4, the reliable OX-5 engine installation being the only common factor. The Waco 4 had a new wing, incorporating the Aeromarine USA.27 aerofoil, which gave the aircraft much improved lift characteristics and it had a forward cockpit large enough for two passengers, and a pilot's position in the rear cockpit with space for a third passenger. The Waco 4 prototype flew in early December 1921 and was successfully used as a barnstormer, however, no further examples were built. The company moved on to use the new wing to convert an existing JN-4 (known as the Waco 4½) for the pioneer aviator, Bill Long. Further modification of three other Canadian Jennies, identified as Waco 5s, combined the revised wings with a widened fuselage, providing space for a maximum of four passengers in the front cockpit.

Up to this point the Weaver Aircraft Company was full of enthusiasm and ideas, but short on sales. Buck Weaver departed to leave Clayton Brukner to sort out the problems. Brukner was able to find new backing which resulted in the incorporation of the Advance Aircraft Company on 10 April 1923 and the Weaver Aircraft Company was wound up the following December. The Advance Aircraft Company was relocated from Lorain to Troy, Ohio, together with the remaining Waco assets, including the partly completed structure of the last Waco 5, which would be fitted with a Hisso engine. Despite the death of Buck Weaver from a respiratory illness, the company continued to refer to its aircraft as Wacos and the aircraft buying public

The Waco 9 three-seater was the first full-scale production model built by Advance Aircraft. It was powered by the famous OX-5 engine and NC539 is an early example.

The Waco 10 was the successor to the Waco 9 and three examples are seen here over the factory at Troy, Ohio.

were starting to take notice of the company's activities. The Waco 6 and Waco 7, eighteen of which were built betwen 1923 and 1924, followed similar lines to those of the Waco 5, but featured new wings with rounded wingtips. The Waco 9, which followed in 1924, was the first model to have a fully welded, steel tube fuselage. It was also fitted with an overhung rudder; extended 'elephant ear' ailerons were introduced early in the production run. Business for the Waco 9 was brisk with forty-seven being sold in 1925 and 164 in 1926.

Though it was externally similar to the model 9, the Waco 10, which was introduced in 1927, was a completely new and more rugged design, with many improvements, including ailerons on all four wings. It also had a new undercarriage with full length external shock struts anchored to the top longerons. So successful were the company's aircraft that Waco's organization and facilities in Troy expanded rapidly to the point that six separate buildings were being used for production.

Sadly, Elwood Junkin had died on 1 November 1926, leaving Clayton Brukner as President. Expansion meant that new senior managers were appointed, including Lee Brutus as vice-president and secretary, Freddie Lund as chief test pilot and Russel F. Hardy as chief engineer. Hardy was followed by E.E. Green in 1928 and shortly afterwards A. Francis Arcier took over as chief engineer and designer. By 1927, with output at two aircraft per working day, Waco required new and more efficient facilities. In 1929 it moved into a brand new factory in Troy, which brought together all the dispersed manufacturing departments and provided an airstrip next to the plant. In June 1929, the company changed its name from Advance Aircraft to The Waco Aircraft Company.

Waco's name and reputation was fast becoming the best-known in the American aviation world. The company's aircraft were being sold to a wide range of customers from wealthy individuals and flying schools to mail carriers and local airline and air taxi companies. Chief Test Pilot Freddie Lund became well known as an air show performer and the Waco biplanes were prominent in every major air event in the country. The fifth annual Ford Air Reliability Tour in 1929 saw a pair of Waco CSOs in first and second place and several special Waco

Waco's story is one of constant product refinement. The A series, represented here by a Warner Scarab powered Waco RBA, N12444, was a side-by-side two seater for the sportsman pilot.

models, such as the JYM and JWM mail carriers built for Northwest Airways and flown by 'Speed' Holman, were delivered from the Troy factory.

Up to this point, Waco's biplanes had been powered by the trusty OX-5 and OXX-6 engines, but supplies of these were starting to dwindle. However, more efficient powerplants were becoming available. Two Waco 10s were tested with the four-cylinder Caminez engine and others flew with Kinner and Siemens-Halske (Model 125) engines, but the principal production variants started to be fitted with the Wright Whirlwind J-5 (Waco 10W) or the 150hp Hispano-Suiza (Hisso) 'A' or 180hp Hisso 'E' engine (Waco 10H). Waco also introduced the option of new tapered wings on the Model 10T, which offered improved speed performance.

With this expansion in the model range, it became clear that a new system of type designations was called for to cope with all the potential airframe and engine combinations. From around 1927, all Wacos had a three-letter designation which identified, firstly, the type of engine, secondly, the type of wing and, thirdly, the general configuration. The first aircraft to use this were the Waco 10 variants (known retroactively as the Model O) and the Wright J-5 powered version with the straight wing became the ASO and the taperwing equivalent became the ATO. Earlier versions of the Waco 10 with the OX-5 engine were identified as the GXE. Numerous other engines were fitted to production Waco 10s, including the Wright J-6 (BSO), the Wright R-760 (CSO), the Packard R-980 diesel (HSO), the Continental A-70-2 (QSO) and the Jacobs LA-1 (PSO). However, the Model 10 variants were finally phased out in 1933, following delivery of a large batch of armed CSOs and CTOs to the Brazilian Air Force.

The Waco Model F, which began to replace the Waco 10 (Model O) in 1930, was a new design with a shorter fuselage. It still accommodated two in the front cockpit and one in the back, but it had a modified undercarriage with an articulated shock strut and a new wing with the new Aeromarine M-18 aerofoil section. The wings were staggered to ease entry to the front cockpit and a much simplified bracing wire structure was adopted. Initial models offered in 1930 were the Warner Scarab powered RNF and the KNF with a Kinner K-5 engine. Only a few examples of the KNF were built, but it was replaced by the INF with the Kinner B-5 and a few of the MNF with a Menasco C-4 engine. The following year Arcier produced his first new design for the company with the QCF, which used the 165hp Continental A-70-2 radial and was fitted with a new undercarriage which did not require the external shock struts.

Despite the Wall Street crash of 1929 and the depressed years which followed, Waco managed to keep its head above water by tailoring models to meet the requirements of the market. The year 1931 saw the first flight of the first cabin Waco, the Model QDC. The open cockpit Waco biplanes gradually gave way to a range of comfortable cabin models over the next few years. The Waco model C had generally similar wings, tail and undercarriage to those of the Waco F biplanes, but used a new fuselage with a four-place fully enclosed cabin, which incorporated transparencies in the upper rear fuselage to give light to the rear seats and a degree of rear vision for the pilot. The cabin was entered through a door on the port side and had a throw-over control wheel to allow the aircraft to be flown from either front seat. The Model C was built with a variety of engines, including the Wright R-540 (BEC), the R-760E (CJC), the Kinner C-5 (OEC) and the Continental A-70-2 (QDC).

In the following year, the company followed the C model with a side-by-side two-seat aircraft known as the Model 'A'. This was aimed at private owners for use as a sporting tourer and, in true Waco fashion, there was a wide choice of models with different engines. The A Series could be delivered as the IBA with a Kinner B-5 engine, the KBA (Kinner K-5), the PBA (Jacobs LA-1), RBA (Warner Scarab) and the UBA and ULA with the Continental R-670. This Waco had an open cockpit in standard form, but many were delivered with a 'winter enclosure' transparent canopy to keep the two occupants in a degree of comfort. These new models ensured continued success for Waco and export sales became a significant part of the company's business, with civil deliveries being made all over the globe, including examples of the Model C to England, Holland, South Africa, Mexico, India, Australia, New Zealand and Brazil.

Wacos had found a ready market with military customers, particularly in South America. This was an important factor when the new Waco Model D was introduced in 1934. The D was a high performance sporting biplane, with a tandem two-seat enclosed cockpit, an upper wing supported by two short pillars just above the fuselage and a highly streamlined spatted undercarriage. This specialized machine, designated S3HD, was fitted with a big 450hp Pratt & Whitney Wasp Junior

As the 1930s progressed, Waco moved from its traditional open cockpit aircraft to concentrate on the more comfortable touring cabin biplanes. This float-equipped UKC-S was built in 1934 and operated by the U.S. Department of Commerce.

radial engine. With potent performance, the S3HD and the later JHD and WHD were acquired by several air forces including the Cuban, Uruguayan and Nicaraguan Air Forces, that had their aircraft fitted with machine guns mounted on the lower outer wings and a rear gunner's position in the back seat.

In 1935, Waco delivered its 2,500th aircraft – a cabin model YOC. At about this time, the standard cabin model became the Model S and the rather ungainly rear window disappeared in favour of a smoother line for the upper fuselage and a longer interior cabin. The company also introduced a new open biplane model – the tandem-seat UMF and YMF, which had a new, longer and more bulky fuselage than the earlier Model F and was powered by a Continental R-670 or Jacobs L-4 radial. To further confuse matters, the designation system was, again, revised, with the first letter of the designation indicating the engine, the second letter indicating the wing or other design features and the third letter identifying the model. By this time, four basic models were being built – the Model F (e.g. the YMF), the Model D (JHD etc.) and the two cabin versions – the luxury custom model C and the lower specification standard model S. Between 1936 and 1938 Waco designations included a number to indicate the year of introduction of each model. For example, the Model YKS, which was produced in 1934 (and became the YKC-S in 1935), was given the designation YKS-6 when the 1936 version was introduced and the 1937 version became the YKS-7.

As war brewed in Europe, Waco produced their ultimate commercial models – the Model E and the Model N. The Model E, sometimes known as the 'Airistocrat', was a high performance, cabin five-seater with a slimmer fuselage and shorter span wings than the earlier cabin aircraft and a wide track undercarriage similar to that used on the UPF trainer. Most production aircraft were the SRE with a Pratt & Whitney Wasp Junior radial, but a few Jacobs L-6 powered AREs and Lycoming-powered HREs were also sold. The ZVN-8 (and AVN-8), introduced in 1938, was Waco's first and only attempt to produce an aircraft with a tricycle undercarriage. Broadly based on the Model C cabin model, the N Series had a longer rear fuselage and could accommodate five people in considerable comfort. The undercarriage was fully faired and spatted with a non-steerable, castoring nosewheel and the tail unit incorporated a small ventral fin and rudder to give additional side area.

Waco's D Series was a high performance tandem-seat sporting model, intended for the wealthy private pilot, but actually produced as military aircraft for a number of South American air forces.

12

The ultimate cabin biplane produced by the company was the E Series. It had a long, slim fuselage and a choice of Jacobs and Pratt & Whitney engines. This is an SRE, manufactured in 1941 and still flying with a U.S. owner.

By this time, Waco had already been swept along with the fever of war preparations. Their F Series of tandem open two-seaters had already proved popular with overseas air arms such as the Brazilian, Venezuelan, Guatemalan and Cuban air forces for military training and the prototype UPF-7, powered by a Continental W-670-6A, was evaluated in 1939 as the XPT-14. It was not adopted as the standard, basic military trainer (that honour falling to the Stearman PT-17) but the UPF-7 still commanded large orders for the Civilian Pilot Training Program. As the momentum of UPF-7 production built up in 1942, with an output of three aircraft per day, the construction of civil Wacos diminished. Eventually, after a total of 593 UPF-7s had been completed, Waco moved across into large scale production of troop-carrying gliders, which were to play a major part in the European D-Day invasion plans. Output of the CG-4A Hadrian, together with a few of the CG-3, CG-13 and CG-15, occupied the whole of the Troy factory with 1,075 being completed by Waco. In addition, companies such as Laister-Kauffman, Pratt-Read, Timm and Cessna also built the Waco gliders, giving a final total of 15,009 produced to assist the war effort. In 1942, C.G. Taylor (father of the Piper Cub and Taylorcraft) came on the scene to co-ordinate the efforts of the fifteen dispersed manufacturers involved in the glider programme. As it turned out, however, many of the CG-4As intended for the Allied landings remained unused and were scrapped when the war came to an end.

With the arrival of peace, the American light aircraft industry moved into the large scale production of civilian aircraft. Huge numbers of Piper Cubs, Cessna 140s and Luscombe Silvaires were built, but the market for the high quality tube and fabric biplanes, which had created Waco's pre-war reputation, was dwindling. Nevertheless, in 1946 there was still a fleet of over 1,500 Waco biplanes which had survived the war period and were officially registered in the United States. The Waco company continued under the direction of Clayton Brukner as a manufacturer of parts for these aircraft and it diversified into production of agricultural and other equipment. Under the Waco name, one further prototype was produced. This was the Waco Model W Aristocraft which was a metal, tube and fabric cabin monoplane with a pusher engine driving a tail-mounted propeller and a Republic Seabee wing. It was a complex aircraft and only one example was completed.

Clayton Brukner died on 26 December 1977 in the knowledge that Waco, with a total output of nearly 4,500 sporting and training aircraft, had been the most successful of all the American pre-war aircraft manufacturers. However, the Waco name has lived on. In the late 1960s, the Waco Aircraft Co. of Pottstown, Pennsylvania, started to offer the Italian SIAI-Marchetti light aircraft designs on the American market. Limited numbers of the SIAI S-205/208 cabin monoplane were sold as the Waco Vela and the SIAI SF.260 two-seat high performance aerobatic trainer/tourer was sold as the Waco TS.250-3 Meteor.

The true resurrection of the Waco designs, however, was initiated by The Waco Classic Aircraft Co. of Lansing, Michigan, who returned the YMF to production in 1985. These new build Wacos are faithful to the quality standards set by Clayton Brukner and his colleagues from Troy. Over ninety had been built by the end of 1999. They join a U.S. fleet of more than 700 surviving Wacos which are lovingly maintained by light aircraft owners who appreciate the excellence of these classic biplanes.

Large numbers of UPF-7 trainers were delivered to civilian flying schools for the wartime pilot training program and a small batch went as YPT-14s for evaluation by the USAAC.

One
Laying the Foundations

Clayton Brukner and Sam Junkin first met at the Central High School in Battle Creek, Michigan. Between 1918 and 1920 they experimented with a number of very simple aircraft. They also gained experience through work on repairing Buck Weaver's barnstorming Curtiss Jennies which stood them in good stead when it came to building their own aircraft from scratch. A series of very similar three-seat biplanes emerged from their premises in Medina, Ohio, and the embryonic Advance Aircraft Co. in Troy, Ohio. Their designs owed much to the Curtiss trainers, but they were also influenced by the simplicity and ease of production achieved in the wartime Fokker D.VII biplane fighter. They drew many detailed features from this aircraft, arriving at the Waco 9, which was to become their first successful mass production model. In 1925, the first year of Waco 9 production, Advance Aircraft produced more than thirty Model 9s. This aircraft was unusual for its time, as it had welded steel fuselage construction, but it was still powered by the trusty Curtiss OX-5 engine which had given such good service in the Jenny and it set the company on the path to becoming the most prolific American aircraft producer of the mid-war period.

An early example of the Waco 9, NC3862 (c/n 316), shows the clean lines of this popular three-seat design.

The first experiments by Clayt Brukner and Sam Junkin took place in 1919 with this little air-boat biplane. Powered by a 30hp Lawrance engine, it had a simple boat hull and spoked pram wheels for ground handling, but it never managed to fly.

The next design from the Brukner/Junkin partnership was the Cootie single-seat monoplane which used the Lawrance engine. Intended as an ultra-cheap 'flivver', its first flight was made by Buck Weaver in February 1920, but it ended with the Cootie hitting a rut and crashing as it landed.

Abandoning the concept of the single-seat Cootie, Sam Junkin reverted to the safer formula required by the barnstormers as a Jenny replacement. The Waco 4 was lighter and more efficient than the Curtiss aircraft and had a two-seat front cockpit and a rear position for the pilot and a third passenger.

Following the departure of Buck Weaver, Brukner and Junkin moved to Medina, Ohio, and built three of the Waco Five. Powered by OX-5 engines, these were built for barnstorming and this example, carrying the title 'Safety Plane', was owned by Howard Calvert who was killed when it later crashed at Kent, Ohio.

In May 1923 Advance Aircraft built the Waco Six, which may be regarded as the true prototype for the production Waco 9s and Waco 10s which were to come. Four examples were built, followed by around twelve Model 7s, one of which is seen here.

Another photograph of the Waco 7 shows its two-seat front cockpit and its 'quick lift' wing, which was designed around a new Aeromarine 2A aerofoil section, giving the aircraft improved takeoff and landing performance.

Only one Waco 8 was completed. It flew in 1924, powered by a 20hp war surplus Hall-Scott Liberty-6 engine and had an enclosed central cabin with large windows, capable of carrying six passengers.

Advance Aircraft's first mass production model was the Waco 9. The prototype, seen here at the Park Board field in Troy, had a modified installation for the OX-5 engine, which resulted in the radiator being positioned on the wing support struts.

The Advance Aircraft Co. established itself in Troy, Ohio, in 1923, using the Dilts Warehouse, seen here, as the main construction plant and another small building adjacent to the Troy Ice & Coal Company for welding work.

The Wacos built at the Dilts Warehouse factory were moved for assembly to a barn on Staunton Road, Troy, which was adjacent to the Park Board field where all test flying and delivery was carried out. Here a Waco 7 and six Waco 9s are seen on the Park Board Airfield in April 1926.

This surviving Waco 9, N2574, the former *Miss Pittsburgh* of Akron, Canton & Youngstown (Ohio) Mail Service was photographed at Caldwell, New Jersey, in July 1966. It has the streamlined engine cowl which resulted from the relocation of the radiator and the 'elephant ear' upper wing ailerons, which were fitted to later production aircraft.

'Fearless Freddie' Lund was a barnstorming pilot whose exploits in the Gates Flying Circus became legendary. He is seen here in front of one of his early mounts – a Waco 9. In November 1928 he joined the Advance Aircraft Co. as chief test pilot.

In 1926, it was decided to fit a Waco 9 of the Ludington Exhibition Co. with prototype water floats, designed by Earl D. Osborne. These 'Edo' pontoons, which lacked water rudders, were constructed from Duralumin and they were fitted with spreader bars while the normal undercarriage struts were used as the front mounting points for the floats.

This Waco 9 floatplane, owned by the New England Aircraft Company and seen on the Connecticut River near Hartford, Conn., shows the definitive support structure for the Edo floats with additional rear struts fitted with small steps. Water rudders are still not used. Also visible in this photograph is the handle for the inertia starter, which was fitted to eliminate the need for hand-starting the engine.

Air racing was a vital publicity tool for aircraft manufacturers in the 1920s and this cleaned-up and modified Waco Six, named *Nize Baby*, brought fame to Advance Aircraft when it won the Aero Club of Pennsylvania Trophy in September 1926 at a speed of 107.5mph.

Air mail services were being developed by several operators during these early days and four Waco 9s were acquired for the Pittsburgh-Youngstown-Cleveland route in 1927. These included *Miss McKeesport*, seen here, and others were named *Miss Pittsburgh* and *Miss Youngstown*.

Another Waco 9, used by Pacific Air Transport for air mail service on the west coast, is seen here. The air mail bags were stored in the forward cockpit, while the pilot flew the aircraft from the rear seat. Pacific Air Transport was later incorporated into Boeing Air Transport, which eventually became part of United.

With its two-seat front cockpit, the Waco 9 was a useful aircraft for carrying passengers on joy flights when the barnstormers visited small towns across the United States.

This Waco 9 has been fitted with a Curtiss K-6 engine for the 1926 Ford Reliability Tour, where it was flown by Johnny Livingston. The undercarriage of the Waco 9 was a triangulated structure with a spreader bar between the wheels. This bar was eliminated when a new undercarriage was designed for the Waco 10.

Advance Aircraft entered three Waco 9s in the August 1926 Ford Airplane Reliability Tour. Finishing in fourth, fifth and sixth places, these included aircraft powered by the Curtiss K-6 (left) and Curtiss C-6 engines (right) shown in this Ford Archive photograph.

Co-founder of Advance Aircraft was James Elwood Junkin – better known as Sam. One of four children of John and Catherine Junkin, Sam struck up his close association with Clayt Brukner at the Battle Creek Central High School. Sadly, Sam Junkin was not able to take part in the success which Waco achieved in the 1930s. He died in Troy on 1 November 1926 at the age of twenty-nine, following a heart condition attributed to childhood rheumatic fever.

The other architect of Waco was Clayton J. Brukner. While he was an experienced pilot, Clayt Brukner's major talent was organizing the production and sales effort, which would make the company into the largest American aircraft producer. With good support managers and an iron hand on the company's business strategy, Brukner was able to fulfil the dream created with Sam Junkin back in 1915.

Two

Building a Business and a Reputation

During 1926 large-scale production was in full swing at the Advance Aircraft plants in Troy. During that year 175 Waco 9 biplanes were delivered. Prior to that time, there had been little regulation over aircraft design, but the U.S. Department of Commerce had plans for a system of Approved Type Certificates. Advance Aircraft's Charlie Meyers was concerned that the company's aircraft would be unable to comply. Not only did the structural strength of the Waco 9 receive a thorough review but Meyers developed an improved version – the Model 10, which became even more successful than its predecessor. Initially powered by the Curtiss OX-5, the Waco 10 was developed with a variety of new powerplants when the supply of war surplus engines dried up. The Waco 10 also appeared with an optional tapered wing and was frequently modified to meet the requirements of the company's many customers. The Advance Aircraft Co had its most successful year in 1928 with total sales of 567 aircraft. In June 1929 it changed its name to The Waco Aircraft Co.

An early example of the Waco 10, NC6511, seen in 1929. It retained the separate radiator used on the Waco 9, but had a new undercarriage and many detailed improvements.

The prototype Waco 10 is seen here at the Park Board Airfield in Troy. Claims for the new model included faster climb, quicker takeoff and higher top speed. The 'elephant ear' ailerons were replaced and the prototype had a double-contoured top engine cowling which was smoothed out in production aircraft.

The major change to the Waco 10 was its undercarriage, which had external shock struts attached to the upper longerons at the juncture with the wing support struts. Here, a later version of the undercarriage, attached to a fuselage frame draped in ballast bags, is seen being drop-tested to prove its integrity.

With exhortations to 'Eat at the Old Phila Hotel' adorning its wings, this is a Hisso Waco Model DSO, powered by a 150hp Hispano Suiza A engine. It has faired-in undercarriage struts and lacks the normal propeller spinner and upper engine cowling seen on the Waco 10 series.

The Reynolds Aviation Museum in Canada owns this red and yellow Waco GXE, CF-AQU. It has a modified forward cowling and lacks the external radiator of the Waco 10. The Model 10 was redesignated as the Waco GXE when the company altered its identification system to three-letter codes in 1927.

Seen here is a Model DSO, NC605N, fitted with the powerful eight-cylinder Hispano Suiza engine. The designation included the engine (D for Hispano Suiza), the wing (S for straight-wing) and the airframe type (O for the Model 10). This DSO was restored after several years of inactivity by Denny Trone of California and it now lives in Petersburg, Illinois.

Atlantic Coast Airways acquired this Waco DSO, NC1746, in 1929. The Hisso Waco was known by a variety of designations – initially as the Waco 10-H, then as the Model 180 or 150 (depending on the Hispano Suiza engine fitted) and, from late 1929, as the DSO.

The Waco 125 was a version of the Waco 10 fitted with a Siemens-Halske engine, which was built under licence in the USA by Ryan Aeronautical Co. Approximately twenty-one are believed to have been built and the example seen here is C5461 (c/n 1400) fitted with the nine-cylinder, 125hp version of this engine.

Another view of a Waco 125, in this case C3777, seen in the snow at Troy. The exhaust collector ring and short exhaust on the Siemens engine are clear in this photograph. An alternative version of the Siemens-Waco was also sold with the smaller seven-cylinder engine of 97hp.

The clean lines of the Waco 10 are evident from this picture of three OX-5-engined aircraft flying over Ohio with, at the far end of the line, a Waco 10W (Model ASO), fitted with a Wright J-5 Whirlwind engine.

This photograph shows the Wright Whirlwind-powered sporting Waco ASO, C7091, built in September 1928 for T. Higbee Embry of Embry-Riddle. Painted white overall, it had many customized features including a non-standard exhaust system and increased fuel capacity.

Another Wright J-5 powered Waco ASO, in this case NC654N, fitted with Edo floats and seen taxying near the Queens Seaplane base outside New York.

Waco had a long and fruitless relationship with Sherman Fairchild which resulted in a 100hp Fairchild-Caminez radial engine being fitted into a Waco 10 airframe (X3132). The little radial engine reportedly suffered much vibration and overheating and was removed in 1927 after testing.

Although relatively few were built, the Waco Taperwing was one of the most publicized of the Waco 10 variants. Conceived in some secrecy, the prototype (3287) is seen here in March 1928 with its cowlings removed for ground running of the OX-5 engine.

The experimental Waco 10, with tapered upper wings, developed by Charlie Meyers, is seen here with its OX-5 engine fully cowled and with chief test pilot Freddie Lund in the rear seat. It was known as the Model 10-T and no letter designation was issued, although it should probably have been a Waco GTO. The straight wings were later reinstalled and the tapered wings fitted to a Model 10W.

This picture shows clearly the tapered wings which both improved the Waco 10's performance and enhanced its appearance. This is a Waco ATO, NR13918, originally owned by the CAA as NS25 and flown with a Wright J-5 engine by Joe Mackey's Linco Flying Aces. It is now used for skywriting and airshow demonstrations on behalf of B.F. Goodrich. It has a metallized fuselage covering and a big Jacobs R-755T32 engine.

Owned by Buddy Batzel, this Waco ATO Taperwing, NC915H, was built in May 1929 and used for airshow demonstrations. The forward cockpit has been enclosed, the undercarriage struts faired in and the engine cowling is a narrow 'speed ring' design.

In 1929 Waco modified the undercarriage of the Model 10 (O Series) with outrigger undercarriage support struts, incorporating shock absorbers on the lower sections. This straightwing Waco CSO was originally known as the Waco CS-225 and was fitted with the new undercarriage and a seven-cylinder Wright J6 radial engine.

The sporty look of the Waco ATO Taperwing is well illustrated in the picture of N719E (c/n A-97), a restored example seen at the Antique Aircraft Association's fly-in at Ottumwa, Iowa, in 1970.

Colour schemes adopted by the aerial circus pilots of the 1920s were designed to catch the public eye. This picture of Zebra-striped Model 220T Taperwing, NC8573 owned by James B. Hall, also shows how the main wheels toed in sharply when the aircraft was flying with the oleos extended.

Waco 10s were also known as the GXE, when fitted with the OX-5 engine. This GXE, N903H (c/n 2037) has been re-fitted with a Continental R-670 radial engine and was seen in immaculate condition at the 1995 EAA Fly-In at Oshkosh, Wisconsin.

The reliable, good value image of Waco in the 1920s was given a new dimension with the arrival of the Model 10-T Taperwing. The new sporty appearance was enhanced by aerobatic performance as shown in this photograph of X5673 (c/n A6) seen rolling over the Ohio countryside.

The First Chicago Aeronautical Exposition of December 1928 saw this Wright J-5 powered Model 10-T Taperwing suspended above the exhibit area. Visible below is a line-up of Ford 4AT Trimotors.

This fine picture of Waco 10-T, NC655N shows its distinctive 'Red Bat' tail logo and the large streamlined wheel pants enclosing the main undercarriage. This aircraft is a Model CTO with a fully cowled 250hp Wright J-6-7 engine.

A close neighbour of 'Red Bat' on the production line was NC656N, which is a Waco CSO and by contrast, has a straight wing and the lower-powered 225hp standard Wright J-6. It is seen here at the 1991 Oshkosh Fly-In.

The fame of Waco aircraft spread outside the borders of the United States. This Model 10-T, one of five Taperwings delivered to the Chinese government in 1929, is seen with Gen. Chang Hin Chang prior to delivery.

The racing Waco CTO, NC21M, was highly modified with single-streamlined outer wing struts, smaller wheels enclosed in spats and a fully-enclosed engine cowling. It was owned by Shell Oil and was flown by Mae Haizlip in the 1931 National Air Races.

This restored Taperwing CTO, NC844V (c/n 3230), has the later outrigger undercarriage and was an Oshkosh visitor in 1993. It was originally fitted with straight wings.

This pre-war picture of Waco CSO 'straightwing', license number 515M, shows the partly cowled seven-cylinder Wright J-6-7 engine.

The Waco O Series were popular as floatplanes and NC8588 (c/n A96), a Model ASO with the standard wing, is seen here on its Edo floats. This aircraft has the outrigger gear fittings attached to the forward float support struts.

This picture shows Waco Taperwing CTO Special NC666N, as flown by airshow performer, Art Davis. It has been fitted with streamlined, single-interplane struts and has a modified standard undercarriage with enlarged shock absorbers and a wind-driven electric generator between the undercarriage legs.

The many commercial operators of open-cockpit Wacos included Michigan Airways, which had this Model ASO (license number 490), seen here accompanied by their pilot, Art Davis.

The 1928 National Air Derby was an opportunity for Advance Aircraft to grab some headlines and Johnny Livingston, in the rear seat, carried off the first prize of $7,000 after winning the Transcontinental race in his Model 10-T Taperwing X-7527, c/n A33. Note the special racing undercarriage fitted to this aircraft.

Freddie Lund was the Sales Manager for Advance Aircraft and a daring exhibitor of the company's products. Here, he is seen in one of the early Model 10-Ts, X5678 (c/n A6).

Brazil was one of many overseas air arms to use the Waco O series as trainers. This bright red Waco CSO, F-154, which is fitted with a machine gun in place of the forward cockpit, is preserved in the Brazilian Museu Aerospacial outside Rio de Janeiro.

Scarcely recognizable as a Waco ASO, this Canadian aircraft has been fitted with a fully-enclosed cabin. Powered by a Wright J-5, it was owned by Cornwell-de Percier Aerial Transport of Ashcroft, British Columbia.

The interior of the Advance Aircraft Company's Plant 2 can be seen here in 1927. The fuselages are for new Waco 10s and the V-eight layout of the OX-5 engines can be seen clearly, as can the positioning of the radiator between the wing support struts.

This Waco ASO, registered 5533 (c/n A7), was the winner of the 1928 National Air Tour at Spokane, Washington. It is seen here with John Wood (right) and Frank Clewers wearing fashionable plus-fours.

NC903H is a Waco GXE, seen here in April 1998 at the Experimental Aircraft Association's Sun'n Fun Fly-In, in Florida. It has been re-engined with a Continental R-670 engine.

Three

A New Home and a New Name

In 1928, the Alliance Aircraft Company was bursting at the seams. No fewer than seven different locations in Troy were in use, from the Dilts Warehouse to the Hayner Distillery building, where engine preparation took place. That year more than 500 aircraft were built. Clayton Brukner had built a very successful company and he was a major employer in Troy. The time had come to have all the company's activities under one roof. In 1928 construction started on the new Peters Pike complex, costing over $270,000, on the former 100 acres Krauss farm, on the outskirts of Troy, which had a railroad track and two grass runways. By the spring of 1929 the new plant was ready for occupation and it was not long before Waco 10s were being completed. The move coincided with a reorganization of the Advance Aircraft Company. In June 1929 Clayton Brukner adopted the new Waco Aircraft Company name. The large investment by Waco coincided with the 1929 Wall Street Crash, as a number of new models including the Model F and Model M were being introduced. The OX-5 engine, in the Waco 10, was finally replaced by Wright radials. Waco was truly entering a new era.

The sole Waco S3HD Super Sport was perhaps the ultimate Waco sporting biplane. It was the civil equivalent of the military JHD, SHD and WHD. This picture of NC14048 shows the extent to which the company had improved its biplane designs since the original Waco 9.

As Waco constructed its new plant in Troy, the Waco 10 was making history. Seen here is the 1928 Transcontinental Race Team of Model 10-Ts. In front is Charlie Meyers in X5673, behind him, Johnny Livingston in X7527 and finally, J.P. Wood in X5533.

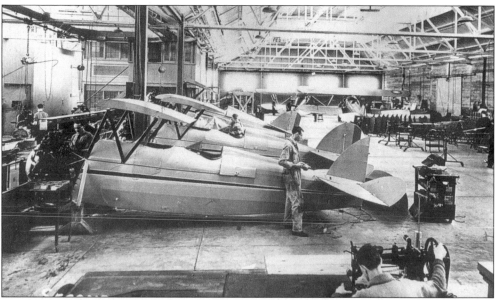

The new modern production plant opened in 1929 provided Advance Aircraft with all its departments in one location. Here, Waco 10 fuselages are seen being fitted with their Wright J-5 engines, while completed aircraft are being prepared for delivery in the distance.

48

The new factory is shown here shortly after completion in 1929. The administration office is in the foreground with a car parking circle in front and two Waco 10s outside. To the left is the railroad track with a spur to the 'Shipping and Receiving' building.

Another later shot of the Waco factory shows the 3,000ft main grass runway to the right of the factory and the double sales and delivery hangar near the trees. To the left of the factory is the shipping and receiving building, which by this time had an additional warehouse on the side.

The Troy factory in 1929 was a busy place. The investment built up over the five years of series production can be judged from this picture of the machine shop, where all the fabrication of tubular steel structures and metal fittings was carried out.

Wings for Wacos were of wooden construction. This photograph shows wing panels resting on trestles during the assembly process. Nine wing panels are seen in production and in the background is a storage area for the wooden propellers, with many other wings stored on the far left.

50

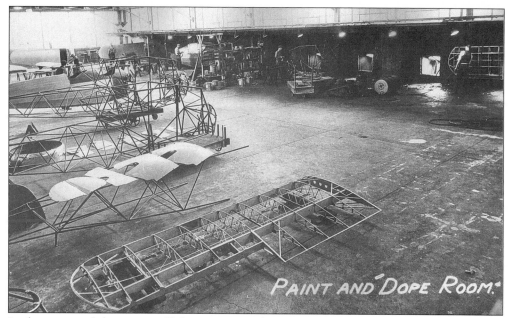

In the paint and dope room all the main aircraft components were painted and covered with fabric. The intricate structure of a Waco 10 'straight' wing can clearly be seen in the foreground, while behind are bare fuselage frames and light alloy panels awaiting painting.

The woodworking department was adjacent to the wing panel assembly line and it was here that the wing ribs, spars, all the fuselage stringers and other components were fabricated. In the foreground is a circular saw for cutting down the stacks of timber seen on the right.

This Waco CTO, NC11211, was powered by a 330hp Wright R-975 engine and flown by Mike Murphy to provide publicity for Marathon Motor Oils. The CTO (model 10T) was further developed into the JYM which had the same tapered wing and Aeromarine M-6 aerofoil section, but was fitted with a 14in longer fuselage.

This Waco, NX8550, is a restored long-fuselage JWM, of which three were built for Northwest Airways. It has the Wright R-975 engine, but uses a straight wing. It had a mail compartment ahead of the front cockpit, accessed through a hatch which was fastened by a 'wire and boot button' closure seen here. This was also used to fasten the rear baggage locker.

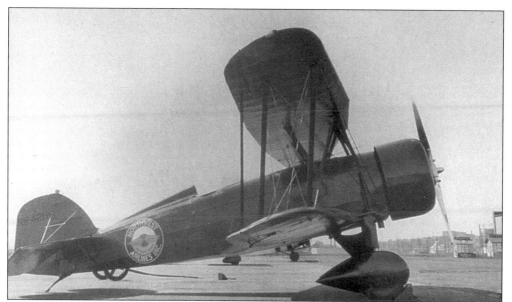

The Waco JYM was mainly employed as a high speed mail carrier by the air operators who flew the Post Office contracts in the 1930s. This JYM, NR42M (c/n 3001), of Northwest Airlines Inc., has an enlarged rudder. Here it shows off its tapered wing and enclosed forward cockpit, which was used for the mail bags.

In addition to NR42M seen above, Northwest Airlines had three other JYMs – N991H (c/n D3), NC631N (c/n J3183) and this aircraft, N731K (c/n D2). It was rebuilt after the war with an open front cockpit and is seen here at Camden, South Carolina, in May 1968 in Northwest's black and orange colour scheme.

The year 1930 saw the introduction of the Waco F Series. This is the prototype of the F Series, licence number 652N (c/n X3197), which started as an INF with a Kinner engine and later became an RNF after fitment of a Warner Scarab engine. It has the original elevator without balanced tips and high pressure tyres.

The Waco Ten (O Series) was gradually removed from the product line to be replaced by the F Series. It was a lighter weight economy model with a shorter fuselage, but still with the two-seat forward cockpit and single rear pilot's position. This is a Kinner B-5 engined Waco INF, N619Y (c/n 3364), seen in 1953 in Los Angeles.

This view of Waco INF, NC11267 clearly shows the five cylinders of the Kinner B-5 engine. Several engine options were available, including the Kinner K-5 in the 100hp KNF, Kinner B-5 in the 125hp INF, the 125hp Menasco C-4 in the MNF and the 110hp Warner Scarab in the RNF.

Another view of NC11267 shows the remodelled undercarriage used on the INF and the complicated geometry of the rearward-sloping wing support struts and interconnection of the upper and lower ailerons.

Waco produced a small number of the Model MNF. Most of the F Series had radial engines and the 125hp Menasco C4 four-cylinder inverted in-line engine in the MNF gave the aircraft quite a different appearance.

Another shot of a Waco MNF shows the centre section cut-out in the trailing edge of the upper wing, which was designed to ease entry to the front seats. This aircraft, NC11246, is fitted with navigation lights for night flying and a landing light at the base of the interplane struts.

This Waco INF, NC11260 (c/n 3409) is seen in March 1950 at its base at Old Star Airport, Langhorne, Pennsylvania. Painted in a red and silver colour scheme it shows plainly the ailerons on all four wings and the extended tips of the balanced elevator surface.

Proof of the longevity of Wacos is this seventy year old model RNF, N110Y (c/n 3298), seen at the Sun'n Fun Fly-In in April 2000. Powered by a 145hp Warner radial, it is owned by David Roberts and it now lives in Greensboro, North Carolina.

NC11264 is a model RNF (c/n 3464). It is typical of the many wonderful Waco restorations and is seen at the Oshkosh EAA Fly-In in August, 1982. The Scarab engine is fitted with the optional 'speed ring' cowling and this RNF has faired-in undercarriage struts.

Only one Waco ENF was produced. It was modified by the Glenn L. Martin Company who married a 120hp Martin 333 engine to an 'F' airframe. Originally registered NC666Y (c/n 3379), it is seen here as N876Z at Spamer's Airport near Baltimore in March 1965.

For the 1931 sales year, Waco announced a new version of the model F. This QCF was substantially modified with a new Clark-Y wing aerofoil section. Seen here is QCF prototype, NX11241, piloted by retired USAF Lt. Colonel 'Curly' Havelaar.

This Waco QCF, NC11455 (c/n 3540) is fitted with the highly polished speed cowling which was an option and it displays the local license number, P748, issued by the State of Pennsylvania, on the fin.

Seen here is a PCF powered by a 170hp Jacobs LA-1 engine. This carries one of the NS registrations applied to government aircraft (NS12439) in view of its ownership by the Aeronautical Department of the Commonwealth of Pennsylvania.

NC11482 is a Waco QCF (c/n 3562) which was built in 1931 and restored in 1989 to the excellent condition seen here. It shows the new undercarriage introduced on this model which dispensed with the outrigger shock strut bracing of earlier Wacos in favour of transverse bracing between the main legs.

This green and cream Waco QCF-2, NC12428 (c/n 3569), was built in November 1931 and delivered to Mid-West Airways Corporation of Aurora, Illinois. Restored in 1992 by John Halterman and powered by a 220hp Continental W-670 engine , it was the Silver Age Champion at the 1992 Oshkosh Fly-In.

Typical of many exported Wacos is LV-RLO, an Argentine-owned QCF-2. This aircraft no longer has the narrow engine cowling which was a normal fitment on this model.

Seen at the Waco factory in October 1931 is this trio with a QCF-2, NC11496, in the centre. On the left is a Waco RNF (NC11456) and on the right the prototype of the first cabin Waco OEC, X12440.

This Waco UBF-2, NC13419, flown in airshows by Bob St Jock of Burlington, Vermont, is fitted with the adjustable pitch metal propeller which was offered as an option on this model. The UBF was a high performance version of the QCF with a modified wing section and a Continental R-670 engine.

This immaculate Waco UBF, NC13027 (c/n 3660) was built in June 1932 and is seen here forty-seven years later in the antiques park at Oshkosh, following a major restoration in 1992. Originally delivered in single-seat configuration, it now has tandem cockpits.

This beautifully restored Waco UBF, NC13074 (c/n 3691), seen at Santa Ynez, California in 1991, shows the rather short nose and narrow engine speed ring which characterized the early F Series models.

Waco's Model A, introduced in 1932, was a substantially new design, based on the earlier open-cockpit models using the B wing, but with a side-by-side two seat cabin. Only twenty-three were built and the prototype for the complete A series, X12435, is seen here outside the delivery hangar at the Waco plant.

This is one of three production IBAs with the Kinner B-5 engine. N12453 (c/n 3603) left the factory in 1932 and is still in service. Evident in this 1972 view is the streamlined nose cowling with five-cylinder heads protruding and the propeller spinner and wheel spats which added to its speed performance.

Several different engine options were offered on the Waco A Series. This is an example of the RBA, which was powered by the 125hp Warner Scarab seven-cylinder radial engine. The pilot is visible in the cockpit correctly dressed with a trilby hat!

Another Waco RBA, N12444, seen here at a Fly-In at Ottumwa, Iowa in 1971, shows the engine ventilation louvres at the rear of the cowling and the drop-down entry door to ease access to the side-by-side cockpit.

The 1932 Waco Model A was a sporting machine for wealthy owners, but it offered a higher standard of comfort than had been available hitherto. This view of NC13067 shows clearly the optional cockpit canopy available on the Waco UBA.

The UBA was the most powerful of the A Series and was powered by a 210hp Continental R-670 engine. Another shot of NC13067 shows clearly the flat panel construction of the sliding cabin enclosure.

Flying over the Ohio countryside in 1932 is Waco PBA, NC12445 (c/n 3597). This model was powered by a 170hp Jacobs LA-1 engine. It is thought that ten were completed.

NC12445 survived the war and is seen here in October 1973 at Jaffery, New Hampshire in a fresh red and black colour scheme. The Waco A was an ideal touring aircraft for two people with its large baggage compartments fore and aft of the cockpit.

The mid-1930s saw Waco developing the S3HD which was a very high performance model, powered by a 420hp Pratt & Whitney Wasp Junior engine, with an enclosed tandem seat cockpit. The sole civil aircraft, NC14048, was built for Miles Vernon of Long Island.

Having fallen into disrepair after the war, the unique S3HD, NC14048 (c/n 3814) was rebuilt by Ernie Webb for the new owner, John Church. It is seen here in October 1975 in its black and yellow livery at Jaffery, New Hampshire, where it is the sole surviving model D and is now owned by Richard C. Jackson.

Waco's S3HD led to a range of military models including the JHD (330hp Wright R-975E-1), SHD (400-450hp Wasp Junior) and WHD (420hp R-975E-3). This is the sole WHD (c/n 3837) with a raised tailplane, wing-mounted guns, a rear machine gun position and belly-mounted bomb racks.

One example of the SH3D-A was built for sale to the Air Force of Cuba's General Batista. This aircraft (c/n 3954) is seen here before delivery and was powered by a Pratt & Whitney Junior SB engine.

Nicaragua was another military purchaser of the D Series. These two WHDs photographed at Troy have wing-mounted guns and a knee-level observation window for the front cockpit. Curiously, the rear aircraft has a non-standard 'blistered' engine cowling.

A batch of six JHDs was delivered by Waco to the Uruguayan Air Force at a unit price of around $28,000. This dark green aircraft is Serial Number 6 (c/n 3837) and it was fitted with a Wright R-975E-1 engine, bomb racks and a single starboard wing gun.

Four
Into the Cabin Era

As prosperity returned after the crisis of the Depression, Waco found that their traditional customers sporting goggles and flying overalls were giving way to new buyers who demanded greater comfort and utility from their private aircraft. Modern airliners were plying the air routes and businessmen pilots could see the advantage of a personal aircraft for business trips and for recreational flying, but without the inconvenience of wind blowing in the hair of their coiffured passengers or themselves. This meant that Waco moved gradually into production of a series of four-seat models with completely enclosed cabins. The prototype Model QDC was unveiled in 1931 and it immediately attracted substantial orders as a result of its excellent all-round visibility and good takeoff and landing performance. As the years went by, the cabin Wacos were progressively refined, culminating in the elegant Model SRE of 1940. The Waco C and S series were put to work with bush operators in the wilds of Canada and Alaska, equipped several air forces and were operated on wheels, skis or floats. They ensured that Waco would maintain its leading role in U.S. civil aviation in the years approaching the Second World War.

One of the first of the cabin Wacos was the UIC. NC13562 is an active example, seen here at the Sun'n Fun Fly-In in Florida.

The prototype Model C cabin Waco was X11250, seen here outside the administration offices at Troy. Structurally, it was similar to the F Series, with a wider fuselage centre section, modified to provide a slab-sided cabin with an entry door over the port lower wing.

With its short stubby nose and boxy cabin, the early 1931 QDC was more in the 'lovable' than the 'beautiful' category. This QDC, NC12438 (c/n 3579), was rescued from a barn in California by Al Buchner and restored in 1982, complete with the unusual pointed rear window unique to this model.

The 1932 version of the Waco QDC was dubbed the UEC and incorporated a number of improvements as seen on NC12474 and NC12440. Notably, the engine was upgraded from the QDC's 165hp Continental A-70-2 to the 210hp Continental R-670.

The UEC retained the stepped rear window of the QDC, as seen here on NC13050 (c/n 3678), but had a new wing structure with the wire bracing replaced by a single transverse strut on each side, which gave rise to the second letter E in the designation.

NC12464 is a Waco UEC seen here in the colours of Standard Oil of Ohio ('Sohio'). The oil companies were enthusiastic users of light aircraft, which were employed on a variety of tasks including visiting customers and oil drilling sites.

The Waco UIC was the 1933 version of the C Series and this example, NC13402 (c/n 3748), was used to test the revolutionary radio compass developed by inventor William P. Lear. The large direction-finding loop antenna for the compass can be seen just ahead of the rear window.

The UIC featured further changes, including a larger blistered cowling for the 210hp Continental R-670 engine, but the major change was the new rear vision window which provided a more elegant line to the upper fuselage. This UIC is the New Zealand registered ZK-ALG.

Many examples of the Waco UIC were equipped with Edo metal floats such as this Canadian aircraft, CF-AVL.

When fitted with floats, the Waco UIC had to be modified with a new vertical tail to give extra side area. This was larger than the standard tail and incorporated a prominent ventral section and a deeper rudder than that used on the land variant.

The Waco UIC was an ideal recreational aircraft and was popular with private owners. NC13439 (c/n 3798) is seen here at the coast of Long Island Sound in 1946. A bronzed swimmer can be seen in the water near the rear of the float.

Dutch businessman pilot Mr. M.A.G. van de Leeuw acquired this appropriately registered Waco UIC, PH-MAG (c/n 3790) in October 1933. As a director of the Van Nelle coffee company he used the Waco for business trips around Europe.

Seen in this picture, in its sparkling red and white colour scheme, is *Texaco-18*, NC13577, of the Texas Oil Co. This aircraft has the wide speedbrake flaps which were installed between the interplane struts on later versions of the UIC.

Further improvements for the 1934 model year, including a small change to the shape of the vertical tail, resulted in the UKC of which NC14000 is typical. For 1935 the designation changed to UKC-S to differentiate the standard model C from the new custom models.

Canada was a good market for Waco and this UKC, CF-AVR, carries the title of the Imperial Tobacco Company of Canada and the name *Miss Sweet Caporal* in honour of a cigarette brand. It has the larger blistered engine cowling introduced on the UIC and the large wheel fairings.

In 1935 the Waco C Series was split into standard (UKC and YKC) and custom (CUC and YOC) models. The custom versions, such as this YOC, NC14615, had a modified rear fuselage with side windows in place of the upper fuselage rear view window, a new undercarriage and a shorter-span lower wing.

The custom cabin Waco had a larger cabin than the standard model and this increased its appeal as a bush aircraft. This Canadian YOC is fitted with skis and is seen in the winter chill being readied for a hard day of flying the mail.

Seen here at the Waco factory field is the prototype custom cabin Waco, NC14613 (c/n 3952), with a modified full cantilever undercarriage without the rear bracing struts.

The Waco CUC, PH-VDL (c/n 4303), was a new aircraft acquired by the Dutch businessman, Mr van der Leeuw in October 1935. He was killed in the aircraft when it crashed on approach to landing at Rotterdam's Waalhaven Airport in bad weather in December 1936.

This Waco YOC, NC15244 (c/n 4327), was built in 1935 and is a beautifully-restored example owned by Robert M. Jaeger of Allentown, Pennsylvania and powered by a 225hp Jacobs 755 engine. This aircraft has a useful load of over 1,400lbs, which made the type very attractive to commercial operators.

The cockpit of the four or five seat YOC, which is luxuriously upholstered in grey leather, is dominated by the impressive Y-shaped dual-control column with its large wood-rimmed steering wheels. The instrument panel of NC15244 has modern instruments in the central, polished-aluminium dashboard.

Waco custom cabin models, such as this YOC, NC15234, (c/n 4321), were frequently operated on floats and, as can be seen here, the existing tail unit was retained, but a small ventral fin was fitted to provide additional side area.

Wright Aeronautical Corporation was the owner of this custom CUC, NC15213 (c/n 4302). It was completed at the Waco factory on 16 August 1935 and in this picture carries an X prefix to its registration, indicating that it was in use by the company for testing the CUC's 50hp Wright R-760-E engine.

Typical of the many export sales achieved by Waco is this UOC, ZK-AEL (c/n 4336), seen in operation in New Zealand. The UOC was identical to the YOC and CUC, but was fitted with a 210hp Continental R-670-A engine.

For the 1936 model year, Waco produced five custom models, their designations all suffixed -6. There were two Wright-engined models (the DQC-6 with a 285hp R-760-E1 and the EQC-6 with a 320hp R-760-2) and three Jacobs versions, the ZQC-6 seen here with the 285hp Jacobs L-5MB, the AQC-6 with a 300hp L-6MB and the YQC-6 with a 225hp L-4MB.

Essentially, the 1936 custom cabin Wacos were very similar to the previous year's models, although the blistered engine cowling was no longer standard. This Argentine YQC-6, LV-NAO (c/n 4445), had the least powerful Jacobs L-4MB engine option.

The United States Coast Guard acquired three Waco EQC-6s in 1936 which were operated on wheels, floats or on skis, as seen here on V-159 (c/n 4547), which was based on the USCG Cutter, *Spencer* in Alaska. Designated J2W-1 in Coast Guard Service, all three Wacos were written off in accidents in 1939.

The EQC-6 was the most powerful of the 1936 custom cabin models and its capacious fuselage made it ideal for remote operations. This Canadian example, CF-BDM, is seen in a winter setting with skis attached and with its large starboard-side door open for loading.

CF-DTD was a ZQC-6 floatplane, with a 285hp Jacobs L-5MB engine and is seen here on a Canadian lake. This particular aircraft has an enlarged second rear door in place of the normal baggage hatch, so that freight could be loaded easily from the floats.

This YQC-6 floatplane is seen running up at the Queens Seaplane Base in New York in 1947. For ground handling it has been mounted on a wheeled dolly which allows it to be moved down to the water ramp.

The 1937 Waco models included the DGC-7, EGC-7 and ZGC-7 which were equivalent to the DQC-6, EQC-6 and ZQC-6 of the previous year. Here a batch of six ZGC-7s being readied for delivery to the Brazilian Air Force.

The year 1939 saw production of the Custom Cabin Series draw to an end, with twenty-eight being built. This is an AGC-8 with a 300hp Jacobs L-6. Other models were the EGC-8 and ZGC-8, which were similar to the previous EGC-7 and ZGC-7. The 1938 models did not have the third rear side window fitted to earlier versions.

This Waco EGC-8 was fitted with a six-cylinder Menasco C-6S-4, inverted in-line engine, which substantially altered its appearance. No official designation was given to this aircraft, although it would probably have been known as an MGC-8. It was subsequently re-engined with a Wright R-760E2 and sold as an EGC-8.

While Waco was building the deluxe custom cabin models, it also produced many of the standard cabin models. The UKC of 1935 was considerably remodelled as the UKC-S and YKC-S. This UKC-S was based in England at White Waltham for a number of years.

Compared with the earlier UKC and YKC, the UKC-S and YKC-S were lower-priced economy standard cabin models that dispensed with the rear-vision window on top of the fuselage. This YKC-S, NC14280 (c/n 4234) was the factory floatplane demonstrator and was completed in May 1935.

For 1937 there were four standard cabin models – the UKS-7 (225hp Continental W670K), the VKS-7 (240hp Continental W670M), the YKS-7 (225hp Jacobs L-4) and the ZKS-7 (285hp Jacobs L-5). This YKS-7 shows the new undercarriage introduced on the 1937 models.

Painted in an attractive green and cream colour scheme, this Waco YKS-7, G-BWAC (c/n 4693) is based at Little Gransden in England. It is seen here at a vintage aircraft rally at Thruxton in May 2000.

Waco offered a good range of choices to its customers and each model had various engine options. The YKS-7, sold in 1937, was the lowest powered of the standard cabin models with its 225hp Jacobs L-4 engine and it sold at an economical $5,695.

Awaiting its customer at the Waco factory is this YKS-7, NC19363, while in the background is the double-bay delivery hangar. By the time this photo was taken, Waco was building up its production of CPTP aircraft and orders for the cabin Wacos were dwindling.

Painted in a bright orange with black trim and silver wings, this YKS-6, NC16512, spends its summers giving joy-rides from Eggenfeld airfield in Germany. Originally, in 1941 it was fitted with floats and operated as an ambulance aircraft for Petersburg Air Service and spent much of its life in Alaska and Montana.

NC20902 (c/n 5214) is a ZKS-7 standard cabin Waco, seen here at a fly-in at Newton, Kansas in 1970. It is unusual in having a streamlined propeller spinner and main wheel speed fairings.

The most luxurious and the most expensive custom cabin Waco was the E Series. Named the Airistocrat, the prototype, NC20951, seen here, first flew in 1939. It had none of the 'dumpy' fuselage lines of some of the other cabin models. Its streamlined shape, staggered wings and 300hp engine gave it a top speed of 185mph.

Only twenty-nine of the Waco E Series were built and two were destroyed at an early stage. This Model SRE, NC20961 (c/n 5086), is one of the survivors and it was one of twelve which were impressed and served during the war as UC-72s. It is seen here at East Hartford, Connecticut, in October 1975.

Looking stunning in canary yellow with black trim is the SRE, NC1252W (c/n 5153) now owned by Jack Womack of Jackson, Louisiana. Three versions of the E Series were built (the HRE, ARE and SRE). The SRE was the most powerful with its 400hp Pratt & Whitney Wasp Jr. SB-2 engine.

The pilot's position of NC1252W, an SRE, is illustrated here. While the instrument panel is relatively simple, the cockpit is dominated by the huge Y-shaped control column with its shaped three-spoked wheels and these gave a further feeling of substance to this powerful and desirable aeroplane.

The New York News Syndicate had two Waco E Series aircraft, one of which was this ARE (NC20957, c/n 5083), powered by a 300hp, Jacobs L-6MB engine. The aircraft were a key factor in getting reporters to the scene of newsworthy events with the best possible speed.

Photographed here in flight is an SRE, NC20962 (c/n 5087). The Waco E series had fabric covering, a tubular steel fuselage frame and a wooden wing and tail structure with plywood cladding. It was not an inexpensive aircraft with an equipped price tag of nearly $20,000.

The sleek lines of the Waco SRE, NC58785 (c/n 5155), show how far Waco had come in the few years since introduction of the Waco 10. Sadly, the construction of the Waco biplanes was labour intensive and relied on craftsmanship which was not cost-effective after the Second World War.

This picture of one of the twenty-eight production E Series Wacos shows the refined undercarriage which it shared with the UPF Series of training biplanes and the unequal span wings which contributed to its excellent performance.

A remarkable number of Waco SREs are still active sixty years after their birth. This aircraft, NC20961 (c/n 5086), is pictured at the Ottumwa, Iowa Convention of the Antique Aircraft Association in 1970. It is still active today.

The majority of the E Series were SREs, but Waco did deliver four HREs including NC31654 (c/n 5157) seen here at Oshkosh in 1987. The HRE was the lowest-powered model with a 285hp Lycoming R-680-E3 engine. This HRE served during the war as a UC-72C with the military serial 42-68342.

Five

America
Contemplates Conflict

By 1938, everyone could smell the prospect of war. For the United States, German aggression was a European affair which was best kept on the other side of the Atlantic, but was it not prudent to be prepared? Preparedness took many forms and included the Civil Pilot Training Program (CPTP) which was launched in June 1939 to establish a core of trained pilots – just in case! Waco had already produced a modified two-seat training version of its popular F Series biplane which was targeted at flying schools and the advent of the CPTP legislation resulted in a sharp increase in output from the Troy factory. The UPF-7 proved to be a sturdy and reliable trainer with most going to the civilian schools, but it lost out to the Stearman NA.75 when it came to military orders for the Army Air Corps, even though Waco did produce an evaluation military batch. By this time the factory was bursting with CPTP work and the high production levels of the standard and custom cabin biplanes was tailing off. Waco's last fling before the war took hold was the N Series, which offered a fresh innovation – the tricycle undercarriage. As usual, Waco was ahead of the market.

This emotive picture shows a Waco UPF-7 in its natural element with a solo, trainee, military pilot in the rear seat.

A familiar sight in the late 1930s was the Waco CRG, used by Andy Stinis for skywriting exhibitions. Two examples of the CRG were produced for the 1930 Ford Reliability Tour and N600Y, seen here as a skywriter with Pepsi Cola livery, was flown by Johnny Livingston into second place – resulting in good publicity for Waco.

The CRG, N600Y (c/n 3349), survived into post-war ownership. Here it is pictured at Oshkosh in 1991 with the forward cockpit faired in. It had a 240hp Wright R-760 engine, a very tall undercarriage and a Model CSO fuselage married to new wings, with a new aerofoil section.

Another oddity produced by Waco was a special version of the Model UBF for the U.S. Navy. Designated XJW-1, two examples were built for use as trainers with the Goodyear airships USS Akron and USS Macon. They were carried inside the airship and lowered on a gantry from which they took off in the air.

The XJW-1, 9522, is seen again, showing the hook mounted above the wing centre section. A pilot flying in to join the airship had to manoeuvre the Waco so as to engage the end of the extendable gantry, after which the aircraft was swung up through a large hatch into the airship's internal hangar.

Waco's UPF, which was launched in 1937, was based on the earlier F Series, but was a dedicated tandem-seat training biplane. Compared with the earlier models, it had a new undercarriage with rear-braced main legs and transverse struts. This is the prototype UPF-7 (NC20901, c/n 4659) which was later modified as the XPT-14.

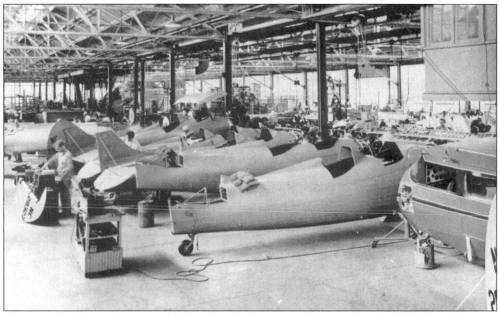

Here, at the Waco factory in 1940 is the fuselage assembly area for the UPF-7, with seven airframes in various stages of completion. One of the last cabin Wacos can be seen on the right.

The UPF-7 was enthusiastically accepted by the civilian pilot training schools and Waco was awarded an order for an evaluation batch of one XPT-14 and twelve YPT-14 trainers for the U.S. Army Air Corps, one of which is seen here. After the evaluation was over, the USAAC selected the Stearman PT-13 and PT-17as their standard, basic trainer.

This is another of the evaluation YPT-14s, wearing the identification code used to spot individual trainee pilots in the circuit. The UPF-7 was regarded as being too lightweight for military use and nearly all the YPT-14s were later passed on to the Civilian Pilot Training Program.

After the war, the UPF-7 became much prized as a private owner type and many of these were flown without cowlings on their seven-cylinder Continental W670 engines. NC29309 is shown taxiing with a joy-riding passenger in the front cockpit.

The UPF-7 is a fairly rare type in Europe, but this French example, painted in turquoise and gold, is based near Paris at Rouen. It was formerly NC29998 (c/n 5495).

This modern-day UPF-7, N30146 (c/n 5545), was built in 1941 and is now painted in a silver and blue colour scheme. It carries the designation GP-1 on the tail, but this is mere wishful thinking as the U.S. Navy never used the UPF-7 and certainly did not issue this type designation.

A familiar sight at the Florida Sun'n Fun Fly-In is this UPF-7, N32122, which sports a pseudo-USAAC colour scheme, but it lacks the fairings on its main undercarriage legs. It has a tail hook for glider towing.

N32137 (c/n 5769) is based in California and is seen here at one of the well-attended Watsonville Fly-Ins. Built in 1941, it is now dressed up in an elaborate red and black scheme.

This pretty orange and cream Waco UPF-7 (N134Q, c/n 5484) carries the name *Spirit of Lander* on the engine cowling. The drop-down door, provided for entry to the front seat, is clearly evident.

In 1935 the Brazilian Government acquired a batch of forty Waco CPF-5s. Similar to the UPF-7, these were equipped as two-seat trainers with the 250hp Wright R-760-E engine and had full fairings for the two main undercarriage legs. This red CPF-5 (c/n 4354) is on display in the Museu Aerospacial, near Rio.

Of the forty CPF-5s delivered to Brazil, ten were supplied to the Brazilian Navy and, in some cases, were fitted with Edo 45-2880 floats. They differed from the Air Force aircraft in having a two-seat front cockpit. One of the batch is seen here during testing prior to delivery.

Similar in general construction to the UPF-7 was the ZPF-6, seen here in the form of the restored NC17470 (c/n 4383), painted in its original Texaco livery. Introduced in 1936, the ZPF-6 had a built-up rear fuselage with a faired-in enclosed pilot's cockpit. The two passengers sat in the forward cockpit which was left open.

This picture of a floatplane version of the Waco ZPF-7, NC17710 (c/n 4650), was taken at Toronto, Canada in 1947. The unequal treatment of pilot and passengers was probably more keenly felt when spray was being thrown up into the open front cockpit!

Painted in a bright orange with black trim, NC29357 (c/n 5384) is registered as a UPF-7, but has been rebuilt with the raised rear fuselage decking and enclosed cockpit fitted to the ZPF-7. It is seen here at the Tail-dragger Fly-In at Rutland, Vermont in June, 1998.

In 1937, the Guatemalan Air Force modernization programme included the purchase of Boeing P-26A fighters and a batch of Waco VPF-7s. This is a restored example, originally delivered as a VPF-7, but fitted with raised fuselage decking and maintained in flying condition by the Air Force Museum in Guatemala City.

As a follow-on to the F-2 (UBF and PBF) three-seat sporting biplanes, Waco developed the YMF which had a longer and wider fuselage, a broader vertical tail and a more powerful 225hp Jacobs L-4 engine. NC14132 (c/n 3957) is a YMF-5 seen here finished in an elaborate blue and white scheme.

The UMF-5 was a relatively pricey aircraft for the sporting pilot. It was powered by the 210hp Continental R-670-A engine and this example, NC14070, is seen after an expensively misjudged landing. It is thought that less than forty of the UMF and YMF were built, including four military aircraft for Guatemala and three for Cuba.

The last of the long line of cabin Wacos was the AVN-8, which was announced for the 1938 model year. Based on the Custom Cabin Series, this model was fitted with a tricycle undercarriage to provide improved safety on takeoff and landing. This photograph of the first AVN-8, NC19356 (c/n 5018), clearly shows the undercarriage structure.

This side-view photograph of the second AVN-8 (NC19372, c/n 5019) was taken at the Waco factory and shows the modified tail unit with its ventral extension that was needed to provide aerodynamic stability. The AVN-8 was equipped with a 300hp Jacobs L-6 engine.

The ZVN-8 was a lower-powered version of the ZVN with a 285hp Jacobs L-5 engine. This example, which is currently active, is registered NC1937S (c/n 5107), but was originally delivered as N19374.

Pictured in its pre-war livery, AVN-8 NC19370 (c/n 5105) has its main entry door open and exhibits the common problem of engine-oil spillage onto the nosewheel spat. This aircraft was impressed for wartime USAAC service as a UC-72J with serial number 42-97425.

Six

War, Peace and some New Beginnings

By 1940 only one thing occupied the public – war in Europe. Americans fervently hoped that they would not be involved, but realists knew that it was a dreadful possibility. The CPTP programme, supported by over 600 UPF-7 trainers, was producing a stream of new, latent military pilots and Waco was in full production at Troy, with little capacity (and little demand) for its traditional high quality, private aircraft. At the start of 1941 the U.S. Army contracted a series of assault glider prototypes. Waco built its 8/9 troop XCG-3 and the fifteen-seat XCG-4, which would become the major production model to lead the allied landings in Europe. UPF-7 production came to an end in November 1942 and Waco went into quantity production of the CG-4A Hadrian and later CG-15, of which 1,607 were finally built. Fifteen other companies, such as Cessna, Timm and Northwestern, were contracted to build another 13,402 examples.

At the end of the war Waco had the capacity, but not the product line to compete with Cessna, Piper and Beech. Regretfully, Clayton Brukner took the tough decision to abandon aircraft manufacture. However, the Waco name was too strong to die. The post-war years saw the name attached to modern, light planes and also to new production models of the types which made the company famous during the heady days of the 1930s.

The smell of war. Waco's PT-14 may not have been purchased by the U.S. Army Air Corps, but it did give sterling service to the CPTP Program and was much sought after by vintage enthusiasts in the post-war era.

The CG-3A was designed by Waco as a nine-seat assault glider, using the traditional wood and fabric construction skills of the Troy factory. As it turned out, the 100 production aircraft were built by Commonwealth.

Waco's CG-4A was a larger fifteen-seater with a braced high wing and a rudimentary fixed tailwheel undercarriage. This CG-4A-GA, 43-36811, is one of a batch of 627 examples produced by G&A Aircraft of Willow Grove, Pennsylvania.

The nose of the CG-4A was hinged to allow loading of a standard army Jeep. One of these is seen being unloaded from a CG-4A after landing in France. It was common for the Hadrians to be named by the troops – and this one has *June* painted on the nose.

In this picture, the open, main-entry door of the Hadrian can be seen just behind the wing root. This is a CG-4A, retained for Stateside training, which was painted silver. Most CG-4As were packed in crates at the factory and shipped unassembled to Europe.

In 1944, Northwestern, a CG-4A manufacturer, produced a service test batch of ten PG-2A-NW powered versions of the Hadrian. These were fitted with a pair of Ranger L-440-7 engines to allow the glider to return after a mission and s/n 45-14037 is seen here.

During the war, Waco's Chief Designer, A. Francis Arcier, developed a range of designs for heavy military gliders and powered transports. Here he is seen (seated) with a model of a proposed pod-and-boom twin engined freighter.

Waco's XCG-13 was a military glider based on the CG-4A, but with a fuselage large enough to accommodate thirty troops or to carry military equipment which was too large for the Hadrian. Two prototypes were built in 1942, fitted with a fixed tailwheel undercarriage. They were followed by three examples of the XCG-13A, one of which is seen here, which had a longer fuselage capable of carrying up to forty-two equipped troops. The XCG-13A had a fixed tricycle undercarriage which improved the use of the nose loading door. An initial order for 400 production CG-13As was placed, although while Waco had designed the aircraft, manufacturing was carried out by Ford Motor Co. and Northwestern Industries. As it turned out, the war was heading for its conclusion and only 132 of the CG-13As were completed. These were ultimately broken up without seeing active service.

In this picture of a CG-13A, the massive hinged nose used for loading light vehicles and mobile guns can be seen. The CG-13A was the last large military glider, and the concept of unpowered expendable aircraft was abandoned as a part of peacetime military policy.

Waco's only monoplane light aircraft was the RPT, which was built in 1941. Conceived as a tandem two-seat trainer it had open cockpits and a fixed tailwheel undercarriage. The prototype is seen here at the factory in its initial configuration.

Only one RPT was built, registered N29375 (c/n 6000). Initially, it was fitted with a fully-cowled 125hp Warner engine, but was later rebuilt with a 160hp Kinner with exposed cylinders, as seen here.

The RPT was also remodelled with an enclosed cabin in place of the open cockpits. By the time this photograph was taken at Ottumwa in 1970, the RPT had also been fitted with undercarriage speed fairings.

For the post-war market, Waco undertook to produce the unconventional Model W Aristocraft. This design, which was not initiated by Waco, had a steel tube and fabric fuselage and a metal wing, but its most unusual feature was the tail-mounted propeller, driven by 215hp Franklin engine fitted in the nose.

The Aristocraft was intended to be a 'family car of the air'. The prototype, NX34219 is shown in this publicity photograph at the Waco factory. The designers clearly intended to get away from the traditions of the 1930s. This aircraft is believed still to exist with a nose-mounted propeller.

The Aristocraft was built and test flown by Waco, but its design was so complicated, particularly as a result of the long drive shaft required to link the engine and propeller, that it was abandoned after much expense for the company.

After the fiasco of the Aristocraft, Waco ceased aircraft manufacture. However, the name remained a mark of quality and in 1966 Alexandre Berger formed Allied Aero Industries and attached the Waco name to the Italian SIAI-Marchetti S.205 light aircraft. One of the Waco S.205/20R Velas, N970WA, is seen here.

More than sixty examples of the Waco S.220-5 Vela were built from Italian components by Allied Aero Industries at Pottstown, Pennsylvania. They were powered by the Franklin 6A-350C1 engine. This example was tested with a modified swept tail installed for cosmetic purposes.

G-VELA is an American-assembled Waco S.205/20R Vela with a retractable undercarriage and is one of a number equipped with auxiliary tip tanks. It was imported into the UK in 1989. It is seen here taxiing in to a fly-in at Moulins, France, in July of that year.

In 1969 the Pottstown factory sent this Waco Vela on a nationwide sales tour. The placard on the fuselage side announced the aircraft as 'The Fabulous Waco'.

Allied Aero Industries also marketed the SIAI-Marchetti built SF.260 two-seater as the Waco TS-250-3 Meteor. These were built in Italy and imported and marketed under the Waco name. N260ME is one of the many SF.260s now flying in the USA.

It was also intended that the SIAI-Marchetti S.210 would be sold in the United States as the Waco TS-250-6 Nova. The S.210 was a light twin based on the airframe of the S.205 and fitted with two 200hp Lycoming TIO-360-A1B engines. As it turned out, the S.210 did not reach production.

The final member of the Allied Aero Industries product line was the French-designed Morane Saulnier MS.894A. This was fitted with a 220hp Franklin 6A-350-C1 engine, manufactured by Allied and it was marketed as the Waco Minerva.

Without doubt, imitation is the most sincere form of flattery and the Waco designs have inspired many copies. This is a Nuwaco T-10-S, N4ZP (c/n 20) which has been built from a partial kit. Powered by a Pratt & Whitney R-985 engine, it is a copy of the Waco CTO Taperwing.

Another Nuwaco T-10 is N813TW, seen here in the antiques park at Oshkosh. This example is powered by a Jacobs engine.

One of the finest Waco copies is this 'UBF-2', NX234Y, which was built by Tom Brown of Unity, Wisconsin from Waco factory drawings. It is powered by a 220hp Continental W-670 engine and is technically in the amateur-built experimental category.

A return to the manufacture of 'real' Wacos was initiated by the Classic Aircraft Corporation in 1983. Formed by Richard Kettles and Michael Dow, Classic set out to produce hand-crafted, new production examples of the YMF. This photograph shows the first production machine, N1935B, which first flew on 20 November 1985.

Built in 1989, N64JE is the twenty-second production YMF-5. Painted in dark blue with light blue trim, it is pictured here at Lakeland, Florida, during one of the EAA Sun 'n Fun spring Fly-Ins.

Presented as Waco's exhibit at the 1992 Oshkosh EAA Convention is an export example of the YMF-5, C-GIBF (c/n F5C-048).

Among the many improvements incorporated in the modern Waco YMF are a steerable tailwheel and modern disc brakes, which make a considerable difference to ground handling, take-off and landing performance. N50YM (c/n F5C-053) was completed at the Lansing, Michigan factory in March 1993.

The Classic Waco YMF-5 is eligible for operation on floats and N42735 is shown ready for launching at the EAA's Oshkosh seaplane 'splash-in'. This factory demonstrator, with standard floats, landed on the grass at Lakeland, Florida in 1998 when it visited Sun'n Fun.

Classic Aircraft's YMF-5 follows the traditional Waco philosophy of upgrading each model and offering excellent value and craftsmanship. The fuselage is now made of improved 4130 steel tube and the aircraft has a stainless steel firewall in place of the aluminium used on the pre-war YMFs.

Despite its classic looks, the modern Waco YMF-5 is built to accommodate modern IFR instruments and a good panel of avionics. This aircraft is based near Los Angeles and is used to give joy-rides.

Most of the production YMF-5s have been sold to American owners, but this example, VH-MLX (c/n F5C-072) was sold to Australia and is based in Queensland. The F-5 is powered by the 245hp Jacobs R-755 radial engine.

Classic Aircraft had built over ninety examples of the YMF-5 by the end of 1999, with output running at around one aircraft every two months – and an enviable backlog of orders. This fine picture shows N21WF (c/n F5C-021) which is upholding the fine Waco tradition.

Ground-up restorations are the speciality of Rare Aircraft of Faribault Airport, near Minneapolis. NX98TW is a Model CTO Taperwing which was built in 1999 under the supervision of Roy Redman and is in reality a brand new aircraft. Once again, the legacy of Buck Weaver, Sam Junkin and Clayton Brukner lives on!